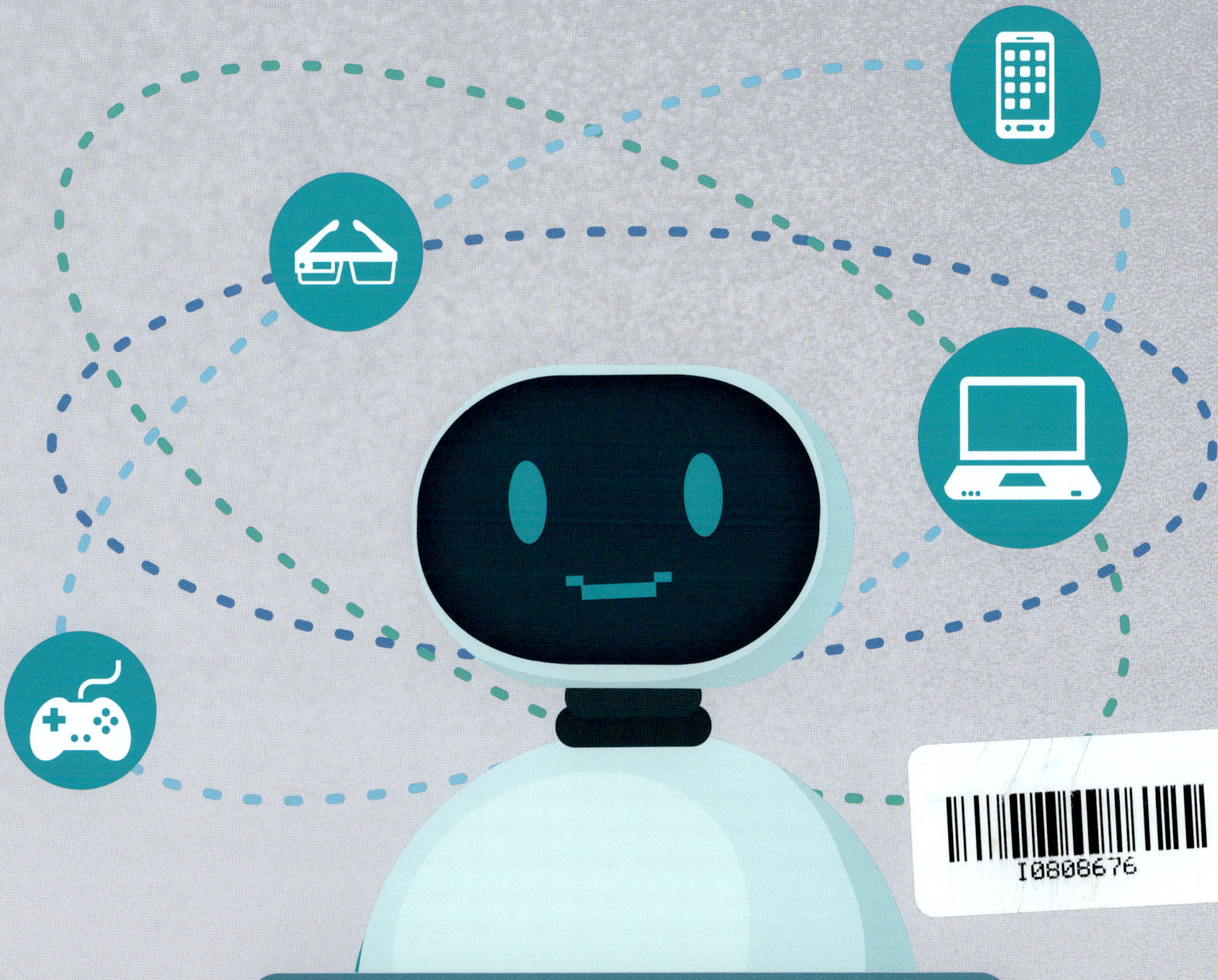

ROBOGRAPHICS

ROBOT HELPERS

CLIVE GIFFORD

PowerKiDS press

Published in 2026
by The Rosen Publishing Group, Inc.
2544 Clinton Street, Buffalo, NY 14224

First published in Great Britain in 2022 by Wayland

Artwork: Collaborate Agency
Design: Collaborate Agency
Editor: Nicola Edwards

Cataloging-in-Publication Data
Names: Gifford, Clive.
Title: Robot helpers / Clive Gifford.
Description: Buffalo, NY : PowerKids Press, 2026. | Series: Robographics | Includes glossary and index.
Identifiers: ISBN 9781499454420 (pbk.) | ISBN 9781499454437 (library bound) | ISBN 9781499454444 (ebook)
Subjects: LCSH: Robots--Juvenile literature. | Robotics--Human factors--Juvenile literature.
Classification: LCC TJ211.2 G555 2026 | DDC 629.8'92--dc23

Picture credits:
The publisher would like to thank the following for permission to reproduce their pictures:
Alamy: Shen Bohan/Xinhua/Alamy Live News 15
Marsi Bionics: 20
NASA: 12
Shutterstock: Bandersnatch 22 (t); elinba 10; Flystock 29; Jensen 6;
Stefano Mazzola 4; Angela Ostafichuk 26; Ned Showman 22(b); Ventura 18
Stanley Robotics: 17

Manufactured in the United States of America
CPSIA Compliance Information: Batch #CSPK26. For further information contact Rosen Publishing at 1-800-237-9932.

CONTENTS

ROBOT HELPERS

Robots are becoming more and more important in today's world. Many are put to work helping people. Service robots work in all sorts of locations – from factories and hotels to cafés and care homes. Many release people from doing dull, repetitive tasks. Others perform chores or jobs that humans would struggle with.

Robot waiters bring food to customers in a café in Rapallo, Italy. More and more robots are working in cafés, hotels, and supermarkets.

The International Federation of Robotics estimates that **68 million** service robots will be sold in 2022 alone.

2,150 ...

... the number of UBTECH Cruzr robots at work in Easyhome stores in China as shop assistants and guides, answering customer queries. Cruzrs working at Kunming Changshui airport interact with **350,000 people** every month.

18,611 SQUARE FEET ...

... the area of windows that the GEKKO Façade robot can clean a day, which is the same as **16 basketball courts**. The Façade has a head for heights, scales vertical skyscrapers, and uses 17 to 51 ounces (0.5-1.5 l) of water per minute to clean.

ROBO-GUARDS

Some robots patrol homes, offices, or factories using their sensors to detect any problems, such as intruders. Many, like Riley, can stream video footage and alerts to homeowners or human security staff.

RILEY

RILEY CAN ...

- view dark rooms using night vision optics
- detect moving objects and raise alerts
- send streaming video to a smartphone

GITA

MEET GITA

This robotic personal cargo carrier from the USA uses cameras and clever coding to follow a person it is paired with around a shop, home, or other building. The robot tracks the person's movement and follows at a safe distance of 3 to 5 feet (1 - 1.6 m). Its Bluetooth speaker can even play music from the person's phone!

INDUSTRIAL ROBOTS

The very first practical robot, Unimate, worked in factories in the 1960s, handling red-hot forged-metal car parts. Hundreds of thousands more have followed, performing heavy lifting, assembling, paint-spraying, and welding in factories. Industrial robots don't tire or need breaks and can repeat their actions over and over again with perfect precision.

LOTS OF BOTS

South Korea has the greatest density of industrial robots of any nation – 710 robots for every 10,000 human workers. The global average is 85 robots.

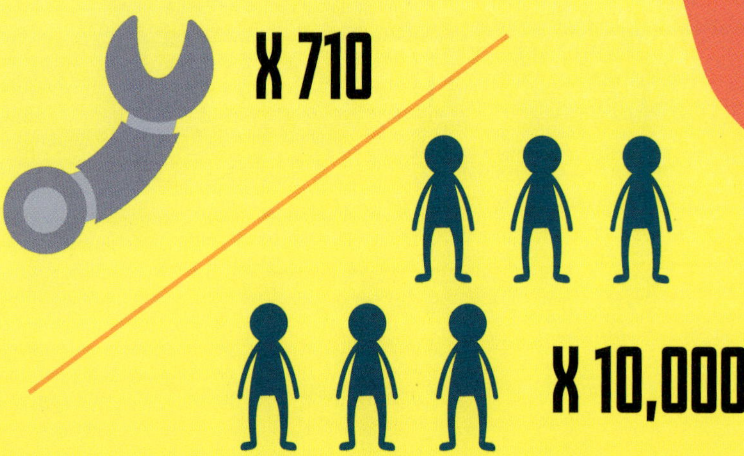

950,000

The estimated number of industrial robots at work in China – the most of any nation.

CAR BOTS

Robots have revolutionized motor vehicle manufacture, speeding up production and cutting down errors. At Hyundai's Sriperumbudur factory in India, 580 robots help to produce one complete motor car **every 30 seconds**.

ROBOT ARMS

Many industrial robots, such as those in a car factory, take the form of flexible robot arms. The wrist joint can be fitted with different tools, known as end effectors, to perform different jobs.

Grippers for handling delicate parts rapidly

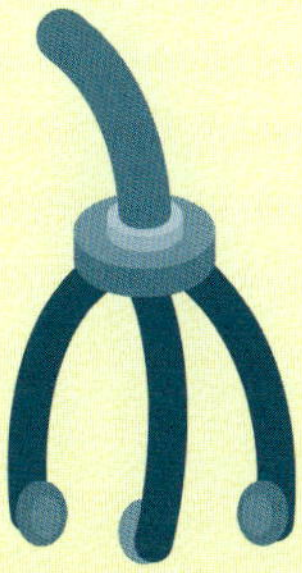

Vacuum gripper for handling glass

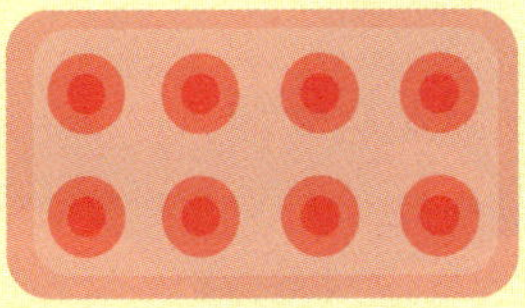

Water jet cutter

Windscreen glass gripper

Paint sprayer

MELTING METAL

Welding robots are multi-jointed arms. They move rapidly between dozens of different positions to melt metal together to make joins called spot welds. A team of ABB's IRB 6640 robot welders can make over 4,000 welds to complete a car body in under 90 seconds.

0.01 IN (0.25 MM)

The typical width of the jet of water used by robot jet cutters to slice through materials. Propelled by a super-powerful pump, the water jet travels at speeds of up to **2,013 mph (3,240 kph)**.

200,000

The number of mobile robots working in Amazon's warehouses. Most are drive units, weighing 323 pounds (146.5 kg), that ferrymultiple shelves full of goods around giant warehouses at a top speed of **3 mph (4.7 kph)**..

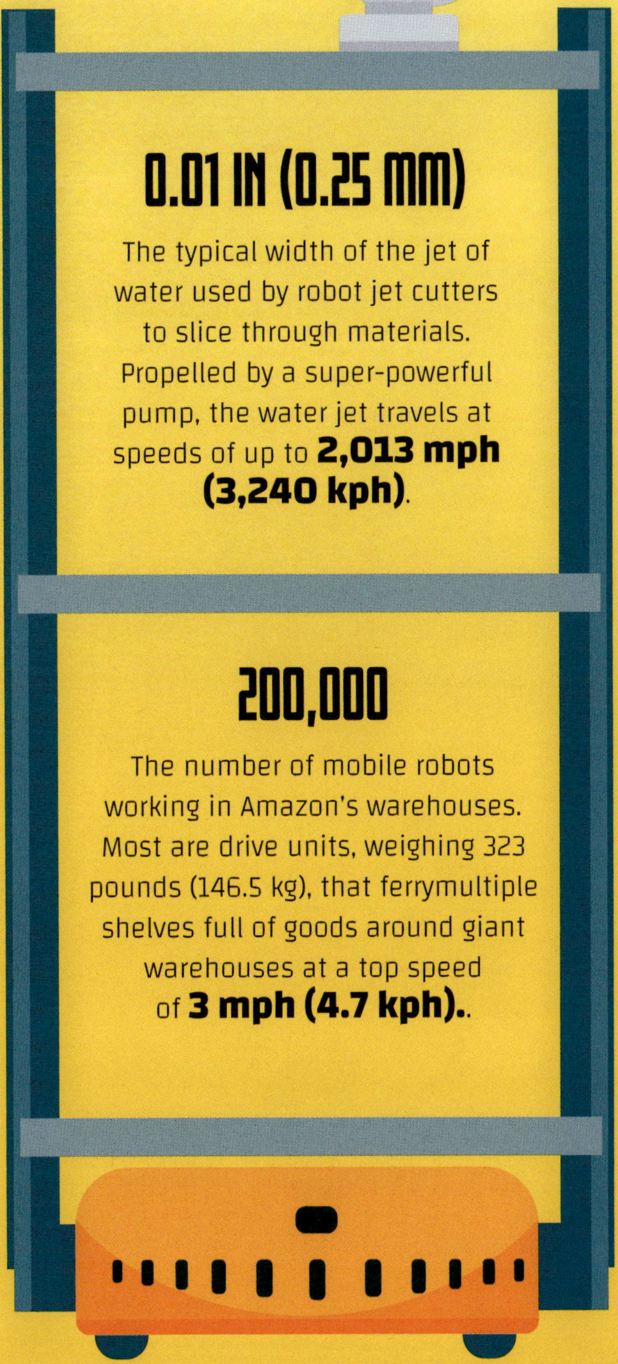

HOME HELP

Some robots are found in the home, where they can inform, entertain, and help out. Some domestic robots are versatile personal assistants, able to control home appliances and remind owners of appointments or medication times. Most, though, remove household drudgery by performing cleaning or other time-consuming chores.

MOWING MACHINES

Much like robotic floor cleaners (see page 9), robotic lawnmowers are 'set and forget' devices which navigate themselves around a lawn, detecting borders, swerving around obstacles, and then returning to their power point when their batteries need a recharge.

The Worx Landroid L1500 can cut 16,146 square feet (1,500 sq m) – an area bigger than three basketball courts – on a single charge.

Landroid robots are connected via cloud computing so they can be programmable by smartphone, detect weather forecasts, and log the amount they've worked. By August 2020, Landroids had traveled a total of 265,139,378 miles (426,700,467 km).

It would have taken people **4,490,631 hours** of mowing by hand,

... has saved 27,000,000 KWh of electricity compared to regular electric lawnmowers. That's equal to the electricity used by **9,300 UK homes** a year,

... and is equal to **10,467** round-the-world trips!

4,755 GALLONS ...

... the amount of water that a Mirra pool-cleaning robot filters and circulates per hour. The robot rolls around the pool floor, removing dirt and debris from pool water.

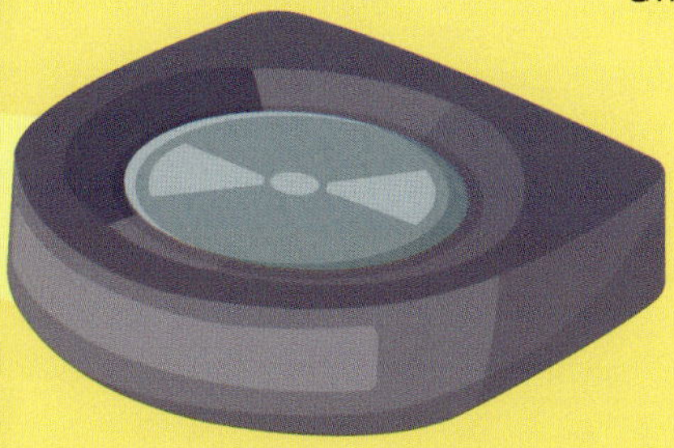

30,000,000 ...

... the number of Roomba vacuum cleaners and Braava robot floor moppers that iRobot have sold globally – making them the world's most common robots.

HOME HELPER

The ASUS Zenbo is a 24-inch (62 cm) tall personal bot which trundles round a home, switching lights off, streaming video calls, and performing other simple tasks.

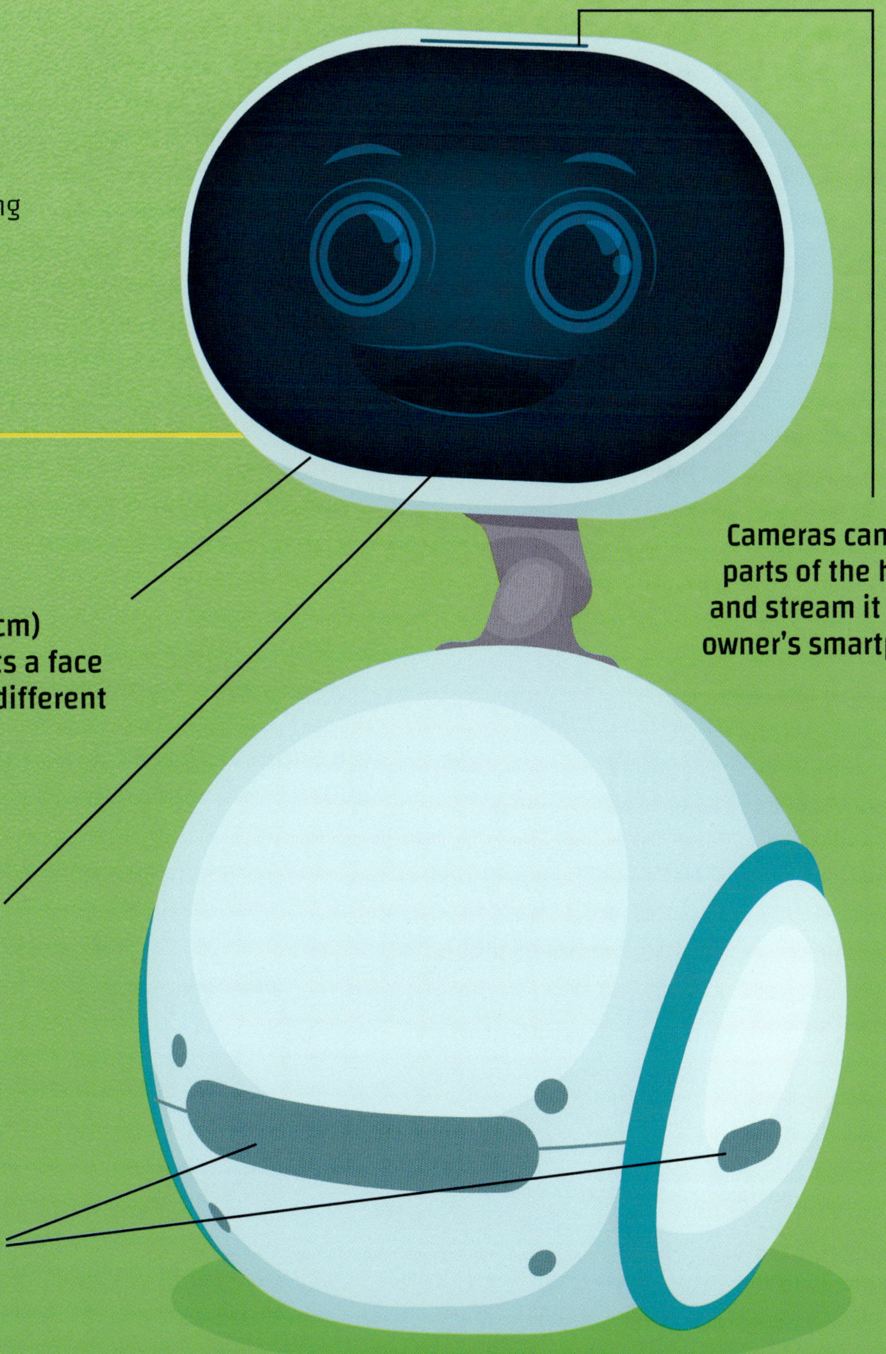

ROBOCHEFS

For decades, robot fans have dreamed of robots cooking and serving food. Now, that dream is slowly becoming a reality. Robots are starting to enter kitchens and canteens where their accuracy and ability to work at a constant rate and carry out instructions perfectly are highly prized.

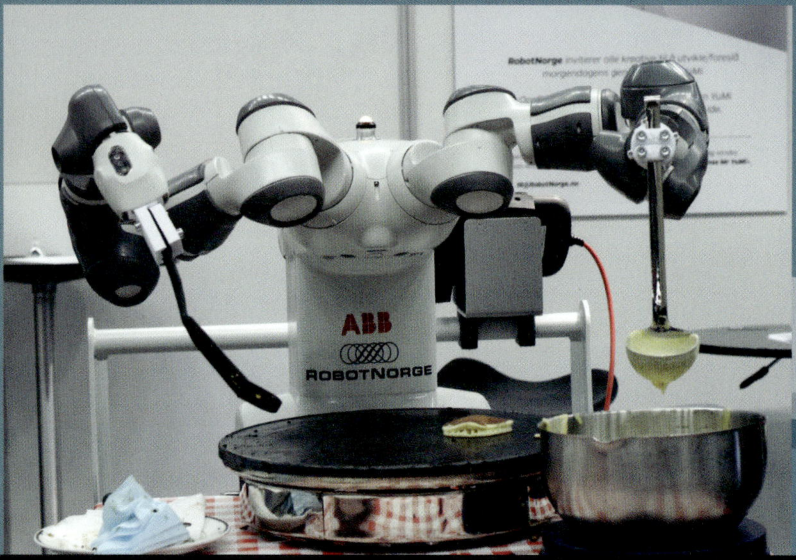

The twin-armed industrial robot YuMi® demonstrates its skills at making pancakes at a robotics exhibition. Find out more about YuMi on page 13.

2,000 ...

... the number of different recipes planned to be stored in Moley's database (see below right)

HANGING AROUND

Moley is an ingenious automated kitchen from the UK. It features two robot arms, hanging from a rail, which can cook meals from scratch. Moley learns each recipe by following the movements and actions of a human chef, storing all the instructions in a database. The robot's versatile, sensor-packed hands can use almost any kitchen tool and detect when a mixture, such as a sauce, gets thicker and stiffer.

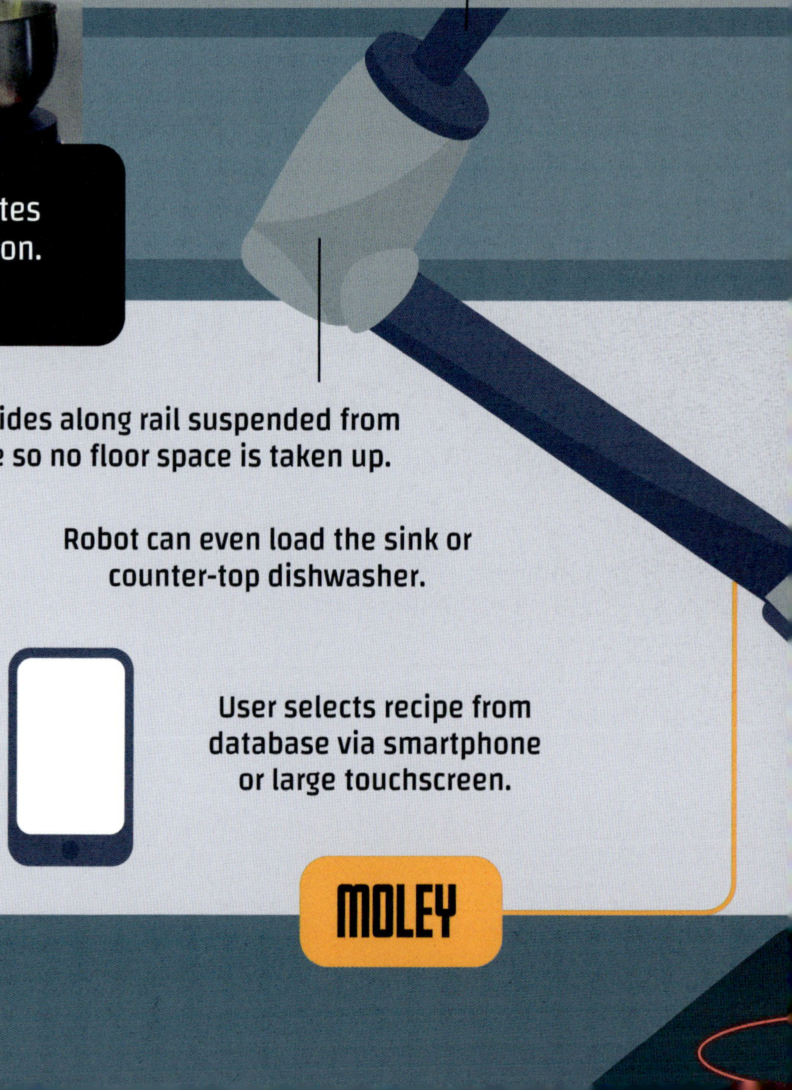

FLIPPING GREAT

FLIPPY

Flipping burgers in a fast-food restaurant kitchen can be dull, monotonous work. Miso Robotics' Flippy uses 3D cameras and heat sensors to determine the precise moment that one side of a burger patty is cooked. It then slides its utensil underneath and flips the burger over.

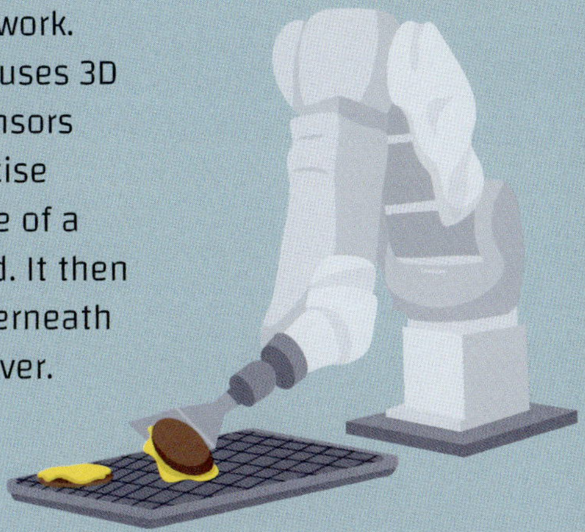

Burgers are just one of 14 foods Flippy can prepare, including potato wedges and popcorn chicken.

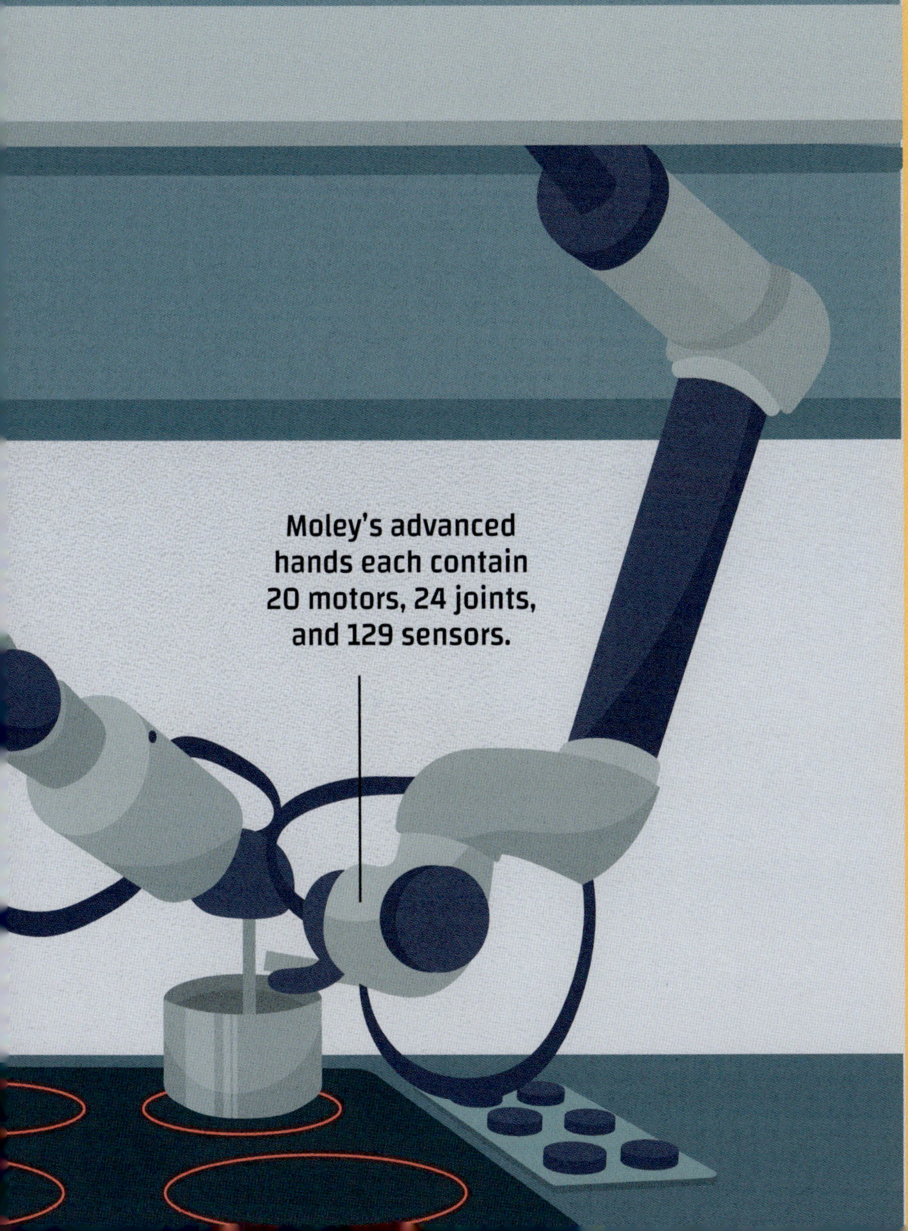

Moley's advanced hands each contain 20 motors, 24 joints, and 129 sensors.

35

The number of different salads the prototype Samsung Bot Chef showed it could make in a 2020 demonstration.

300

The number of pizzas per hour a 2020 prototype robot called Picnic can make. The robot adds sauce, cheese, and up to six different toppings in a mini automated assembly line before the pizza is baked.

Laid end-to-end, the pizzas the robot makes in 68 minutes would stretch the length of a soccer field.

60-90

The seconds it takes for the two robots at a Tipsy Robot stand to make, shake, and pour a cocktail drink. The robots can make **1,440 drinks a day**.

5X ...

... the speed of Ella, a robot coffee-maker, compared to a human barista. At work in Singapore, Ella can make 15 different coffees and recognize regular customer's faces, recalling their favorite hot drink.

ROBOT ARMS

One of the most "handy" types of robots are robot arms. Often fitted with shoulder, elbow, and wrist joints and sometimes a waist joint as well, these flexible devices have been put to dozens of different uses. Many are found in factories and laboratories, but others are used in shops and schools and are even put to work in space.

MEGA MISSION

The largest and longest robot arm currently working is found 249 miles (400 km) above Earth on the International Space Station. Installed in 2001, the Canadarm2 measures 58 feet (17.6 m) long and weighs 3,616 lb (1,640 kg)– more than a medium-sized car.

In space, where the pull of gravity is not very strong, the robot can handle masses of up to **255,736 pounds (116,000 kg)** – about the weight of **18 T-rex dinosaurs!**

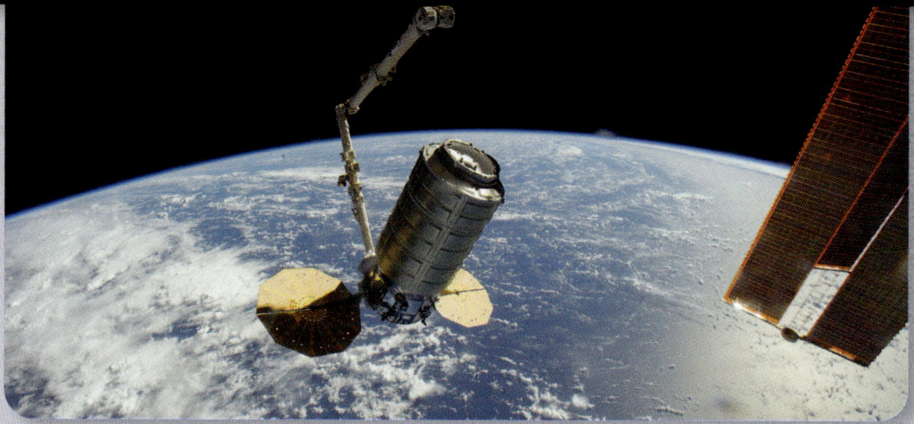

STRONG ARM

Back on Earth, the FANUC M-2000iA is the world's strongest robot arm. Fixed to the floor, the robot can lift objects up to 15 feet (4.6 m) off the ground and can reach out 12 feet (3.7 m) horizontally. Its powerful motors can lift loads of up to 5,071 pounds (2,300 kg). That's more than 1 ½ times the weight of a Corvette Stingray sports car, 101 Gita robots, or 230 ASUS Zenbos.

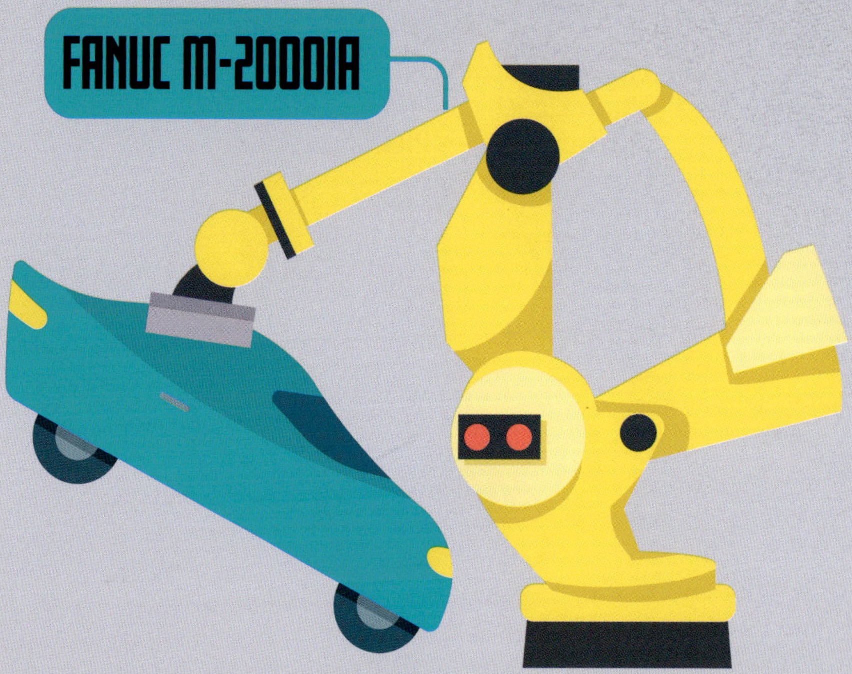

LIGHT WORK

An incredible prototype robot arm made by Japanese scientists measures 66 feet (20 m) long but weighs just 2.6 pounds (1.2 kg)! The secret? It's made from metallic film balloonsfilled with helium gas.

3.25 ...

... the number of seconds it took the CubeStormer 3 robot to solve a Rubik's Cube! The four-handed robot was mainly built out of LEGO with a smartphone as its controller.

SMALL BUT ACCURATE

British robot Meca500 weighs just 10 pounds (4.5 kg) and can sit in the palm of your hand. One of the smallest ever industrial robots, it can perform assembly, gluing, and inspection of the tiniest, trickiest objects with incredible accuracy.

Meca500's six joints can repeat movements again and again to within 0.0002 inch (0.005 mm). That's:

1/250th the size of a single grain of sand

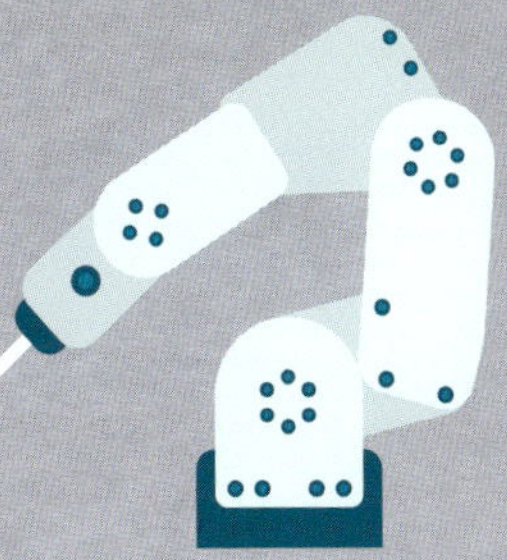

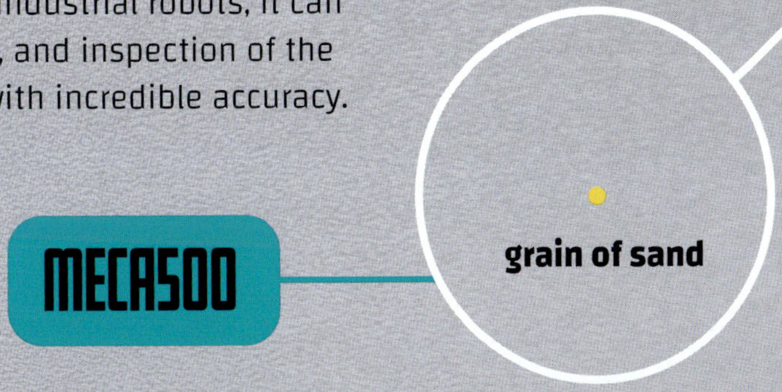

YUMI

As humans know, two arms can be better than one, especially when it comes to tricky tasks, such as assembling smartphones and other small objects. ABB's YuMi has a soft body as it's designed to work alongside humans on assembly lines. YuMi is very versatile and has:

MEDICAL ROBOTS

Robots are increasingly found in hospitals and medical centers where they perform important behind-the-scenes work, such as creating prescriptions, testing blood samples, and delivering bedding and medicines. A handful of robots work with patients, helping to perform operations under the guidance of a human surgeon.

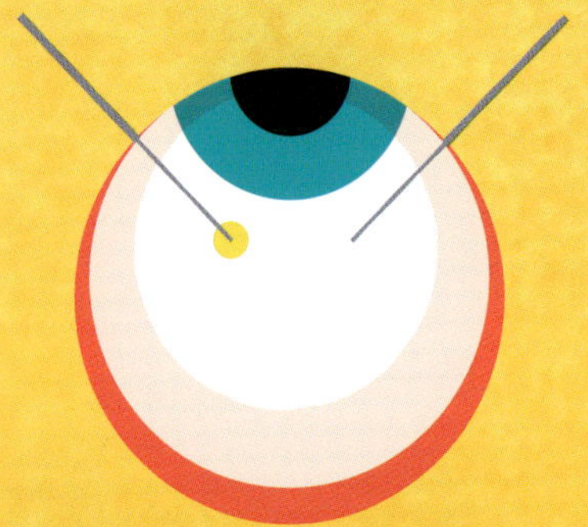

PRECISE WORK

The PRECEYES Surgical System helps surgeons work inside the human eye to reattach retinas and perform other operations with incredible precision. The robot moves the surgical tools to within 0.0008 inch (0.02 mm) – that's just 1/4 the width of a human hair.

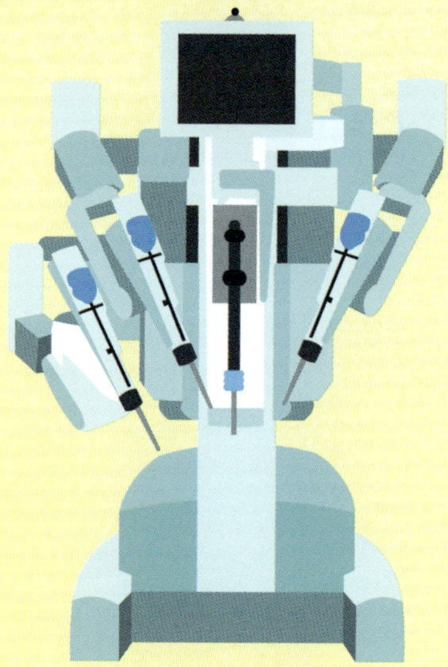

6,000,000 ...

... the number of surgeries performed by da Vinci surgical robots. These multi-armed robots perform operations through tiny cuts in the patient's body.

TAKING YOUR MEDICINE

Robot pharmacists such as Robot-Rx prepare medical prescriptions for patients. Using barcode scanning, the robot's arm whizzes up, down, and along rails selecting the right medicine from 770 different drugs.

A Robot-Rx dispenses 6,000-7,000 prescriptions a day, saving human pharmacists 90% of their time.

KEEP IT CLEAN

Some hospitals use robots to tirelessly clean wards and corridors to reduce the risk of infection. XENEX, Violet, and UVD® robots bombard areas to be cleaned with ultraviolet (UV) light to disinfect and kill almost all microbes.

The UVD robot from Denmark can navigate itself through hospital corridors and even up and down lifts to reach the areas it has to clean.

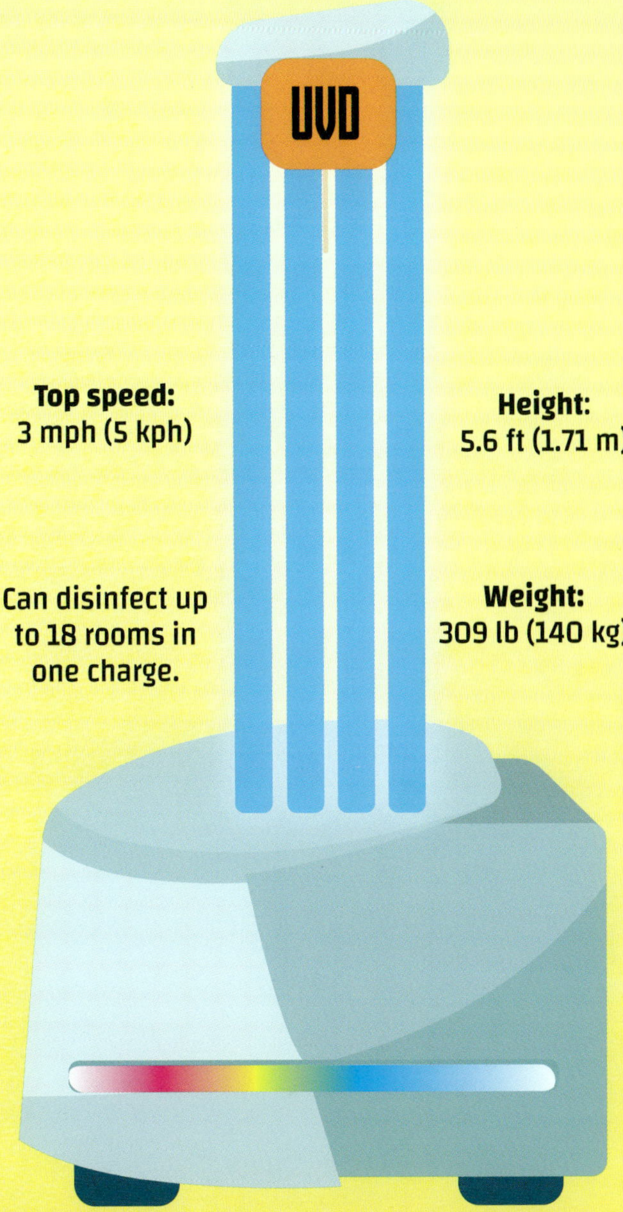

Top speed:
3 mph (5 kph)

Height:
5.6 ft (1.71 m)

Can disinfect up to 18 rooms in one charge.

Weight:
309 lb (140 kg)

UVD kills 99.99% of all bacteria in one 10-minute cleaning session.

20,000 ...

... the maximum capacity of a COVID-19 field hospital in Wuhan, China in 2020. Some wards were staffed entirely by robots, which took temperatures, instructed patients, delivered medicine and food, and sprayed disinfectant (left). The robots helped reduce contact between infected patients and human doctors and nurses.

PICKERS AND PACKERS

Many robots work in factories, tracking items with their vision systems, then picking and placing them as products are assembled or packaged. These robots need to be reliable and highly accurate. Their actions must be perfectly repeatable, meaning that the same task can be performed over and over again without any deviations or errors.

SUPER-QUICK PICK

Delta robots are factory bots, which are usually suspended over a conveyor belt. Their rods react rapidly to move the robot's end effector, often a gripper, to pick up something. None is faster than ABB's IRB 360 FlexPicker, which can lift loads of up to 18 pounds (8 kg).

FLEXPICKER CAN ...

... stack pancakes prior to wrapping.

... place medicines and other products into packs.

... pack meat products into trays.

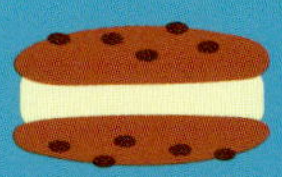

... sandwich cookies together.

FLEXPICKER

500 ...

... the number of objects the IRB 360 Flexpicker can pick up and handle per minute. That's **240,000** items in a single eight-hour shift!

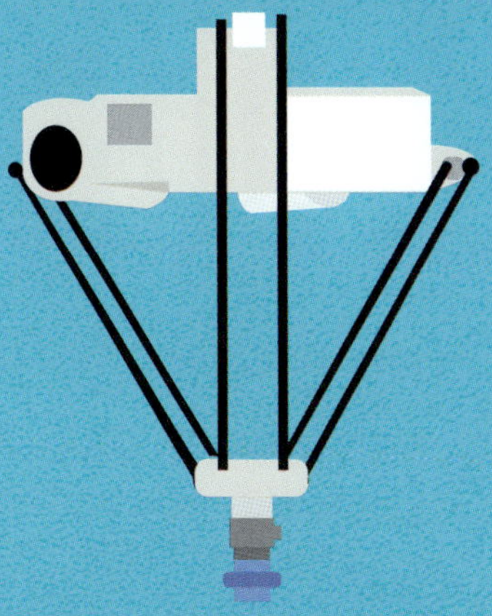

The Omron Adept Quattro **four-armed** robot uses its speedy vision system to identify different-shaped chocolates. It can pick and fill up to **30 boxes** with chocolates in just **60 seconds**.

PALLETIZING

Some robots specialize in heavier lifting, loading packs of products onto wooden pallets which are then sent on by road or rail. KUKA's QUANTEC palletizer robots, for example, load up **44 tons (40 tonnes)** of cat litter packs in Certech's factory in Poland every **eight-hour shift**.

Maximum load: 529 lb (240 kg) – more than the average weight of three men

Despite their heavy-lifting prowess, the robots' movements are repeatable and accurate to **0.06 mm** every time. That's about the 3/5 the width of a human hair.

-30 °C

The lowest temperature KUKA's KR QUANTEC 'Arctic' picking robots can work at when packaging and palletising frozen foods.

CAR VALET

Some robots pick up cars and park them. French robot Stan can park **400** vehicles, each up to 20 feet (6 m) long, with astonishing accuracy. The robot slides its long forklift plates underneath a car and guides it into a tight parking space using SLAM (simultaneous localising and mapping) and other precision sensors.

As a result of Stan's accuracy, **50%** more cars can be fitted into the same car park than if they were parked by human drivers.

LET THEM ENTERTAIN YOU

Demonstration robots first appeared in the 1930s, wowing audiences by pretending to do human-like things. These devices were usually electrical and mechanical models with no controller or ability to make smart decisions. Things have moved on since then, with a wide range of real robots now able to play games and music, and entertain.

20,000 ...

... the number of performances made by RoboThespian actor robots at the Copernicus Science Centre in Poland. That's nearly 6,000 more performances than the long-running musical *Les Misérables* in London.

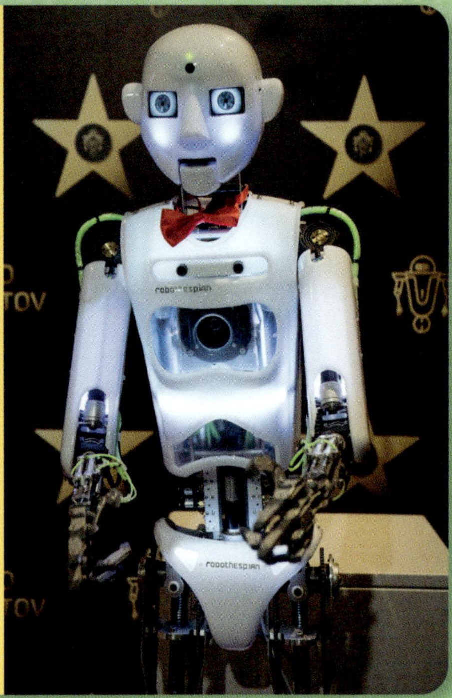

CHEERLEADERS

Japan is home to **three troupes of 12** cheerleading robots called Murata, capable of performing choreographed routines. Each robot sends out infrared and ultrasonic signals which we cannot see or hear, but which enable the robots to keep track of where they all are and perform routines precisely.

A Murata uses gyroscopic sensors to stay balanced and upright.

Infrared sensors: 4

LEDS light up pom-poms.

Height: 14 in (36 cm)

Ultrasonic microphones in head: 5

MURATA

A Murata's top speed is **100 feet (30 m) per second**, or 67 mph (108 kph). That's faster than the car speed limit in most countries. It's **11 times faster** than Gita (see page 5) and **36 times faster** than Pepper robots (see page 22).

MACHINE MUSIC

A number of robots play musical instruments, including Toshiba's 5-foot ((1.5 m)-tall trumpet-playing Partner robot. Few robots rock as hard as two three-piece robot bands – Compressorhead from Germany and Z-Machines from Japan. Both feature pneumatically-powered guitar-playing robots, each with **78 fingers**.

Z-Machines' Ashura has **6** arms, uses **19** drumsticks and **3** bass drums, and can play **4** times faster than a human drummer.

DOGGY DROID

Sony's AIBO robot dogs have charmed several generations of kids. The latest version, released in 2018, comes with a bone it will hunt for, a ball to play with, and the ability to learn lots of new tricks. It can also patrol a home as a security guard, seeking out faces it recognizes and those it doesn't.

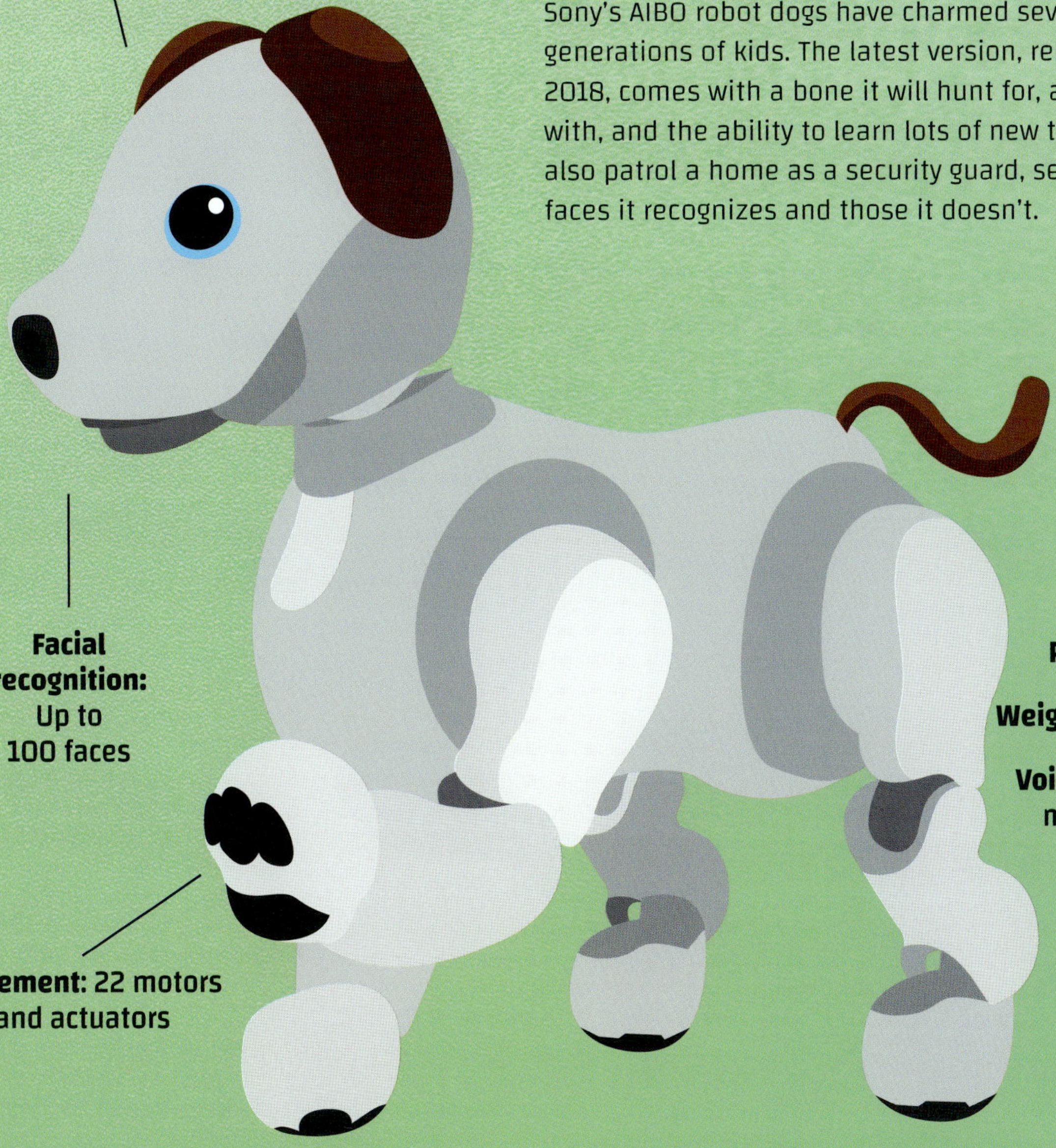

REHAB ROBOTS

Some robots help patients during rehabilitation – recovery from injury and illness. Robotic exoskeletons, for example, can support a patient's weight and assist their movement until they can build up the strength to do it fully for themselves. Other robots can help take a patient through rehab exercises or make their life easier as they recover.

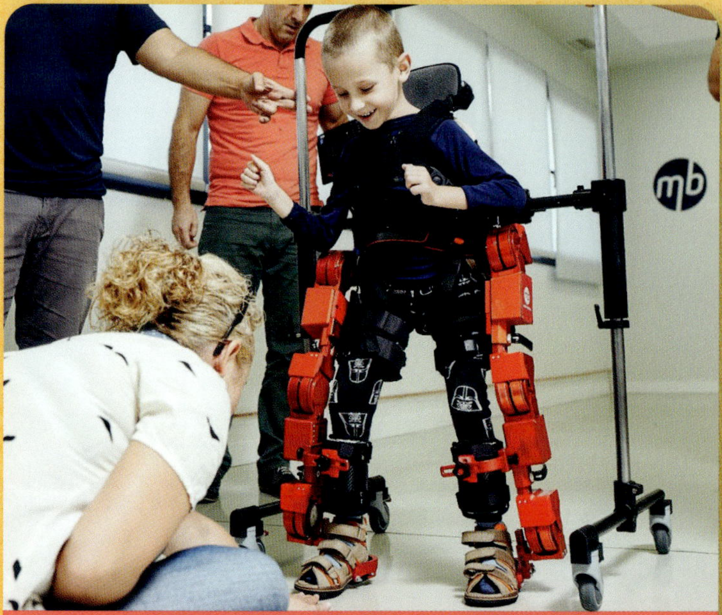

Robots like this ATLAS 2030 support patients as they exercise to strengthen their muscles or improve their heart and lung fitness.

THAT'S HANDY

Many millions of people suffer loss of movement or strength in their hands following a stroke or spinal cord injury. Robots like the RELab tenoexo can help. It is worn on the hand, where its small motors exert pressure at the fingertips. This provides help with 80 percent of all grasping movements.

Weight: 5 oz (148 g)–about the same as six AA batteries

RE-LEARNING HOW TO WALK

Powered exoskeletons with hydraulic actuators or electric motors strap on to a patient's body. They can help balance and move the legs of a patient who has lost muscle or nerve function after injury or illness.

127,994,060 ...

... the number of steps taken up to August 2020 by over 20,400 patients using EksoNR exoskeletons. That's a distance of more than three times round the world.

ROBO-PHYSIO

A human physical therapist guides ROBERT® the robot, from Denmark, through a set of exercises on a patient. The robot remembers the precise movements and can repeat them again and again. While the robot conducts a therapy session, the human physical therapist has time to treat others.

ROBERT

30-40 minutes: typical duration of a session conducted by ROBERT

JUST FOR KIDS

Marsi Bionics' ATLAS 2030 exoskeleton (shown in the photo on page 20) from Spain is designed to support children with severe muscle injury and illnesses such as muscular dystrophy. Strapped to patients' legs and bodies, the robot's electric motors help move the leg joints to encourage walking and muscle strengthening.

Weight:
31 lbs (14 kg)

Fitting time:
5 minutes

Powered joints: 8

Maximum speed:
1.5 ft (0.5 m) per second

AT YOUR SERVICE

Robots are being developed to deal with human customers in service industries. They can work long hours without breaks, guiding people around museums and other visitor attractions, or greeting customers at hotels, stores, and offices.

A robot guide helps passengers at South Korea's Incheon International Airport.

PEPPER

Capable of chatting, gesturing, and interacting with human customers, over 2,000 companies have put Pepper robots to work, many in banks, stores, airports, and hotels. They can guide customers, answer questions, and demonstrate products and offers.

15 ...

... the number of languages Pepper can recognize questions and commands and reply in. These include English, French, Spanish, Korean, and Japanese.

Each Pepper robot is 4 feet (1.2 m) tall and 62 pounds (28 kg).

ROBOT GUIDES

In 2018, Pepper robots became the USA's Smithsonian museums' newest recruits. These robots are among a growing group of tour guides. Some, such as Betty at Blenheim Palace, UK, and Tim at the German Museum of Technology in Berlin, Germany, are based on the SCITOS A5 robot. They lead visitors around the exhibits, answering questions and providing commentaries. The SCITOS A5 can work 12-18 hour shifts and has a 360 degree panoramic camera, giving constant all-around views.

During the COVID-19 pandemic, some robots, such as the Double, traveled around closed galleries and museums, such as the Hastings Contemporary museum in the UK, providing filmed tours which people could stream and enjoy from home.

PEPPER

Three wheels on base can swivel to move robot in any direction with a top speed of 2 mph (3 kph).

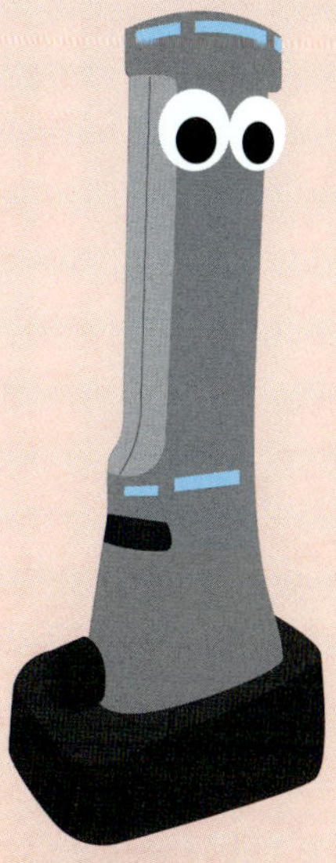

12 HOURS ...

... the length of shift 500 Marty robots perform in stores in the United States. The 6-foot (1.9 m) tall robot uses LiDAR and other sensors to detect empty shelves, spillages, and other problems in the aisles and alert human staff.

50,000 ...

... the operating life in hours of Keenan's cute Peanut. With shifts lasting up to 10 hours, that's over 13 years. The bot can act as a tour guide, usher or mobile ads, holding a giant double-sided screen.

Dimensions: 57 in x 20 in x 24 in (145 cm x 50 cm x 60 cm)
Weight: 154 lb (70 kg)
Speed: 3 ft/s (1 m/s)

SPORTS BOTS

Relax - your favorite sports team isn't likely to be signing a robot player yet. However, some sportspeople are using robots as accurate, consistent training aids. Other sporty bots allow robotics researchers to work on robots' reactions and abilities to predict where they, their opponent, or the ball will be next.

TABLE TENNIS TRAINER

Tracking a fast-moving ping-pong ball in real time is a huge challenge for robots. Omron's Forpheus robot uses high-speed cameras and artificial intelligence algorithms. It calculates the ball's trajectory and how much spin is on it to predict where the ball will head after it bounces.

1/1000TH SECOND ...

... the time taken by the robot's controller to calculate the timing and direction of the robot's next shot – 300 times quicker than a blink of an eye!

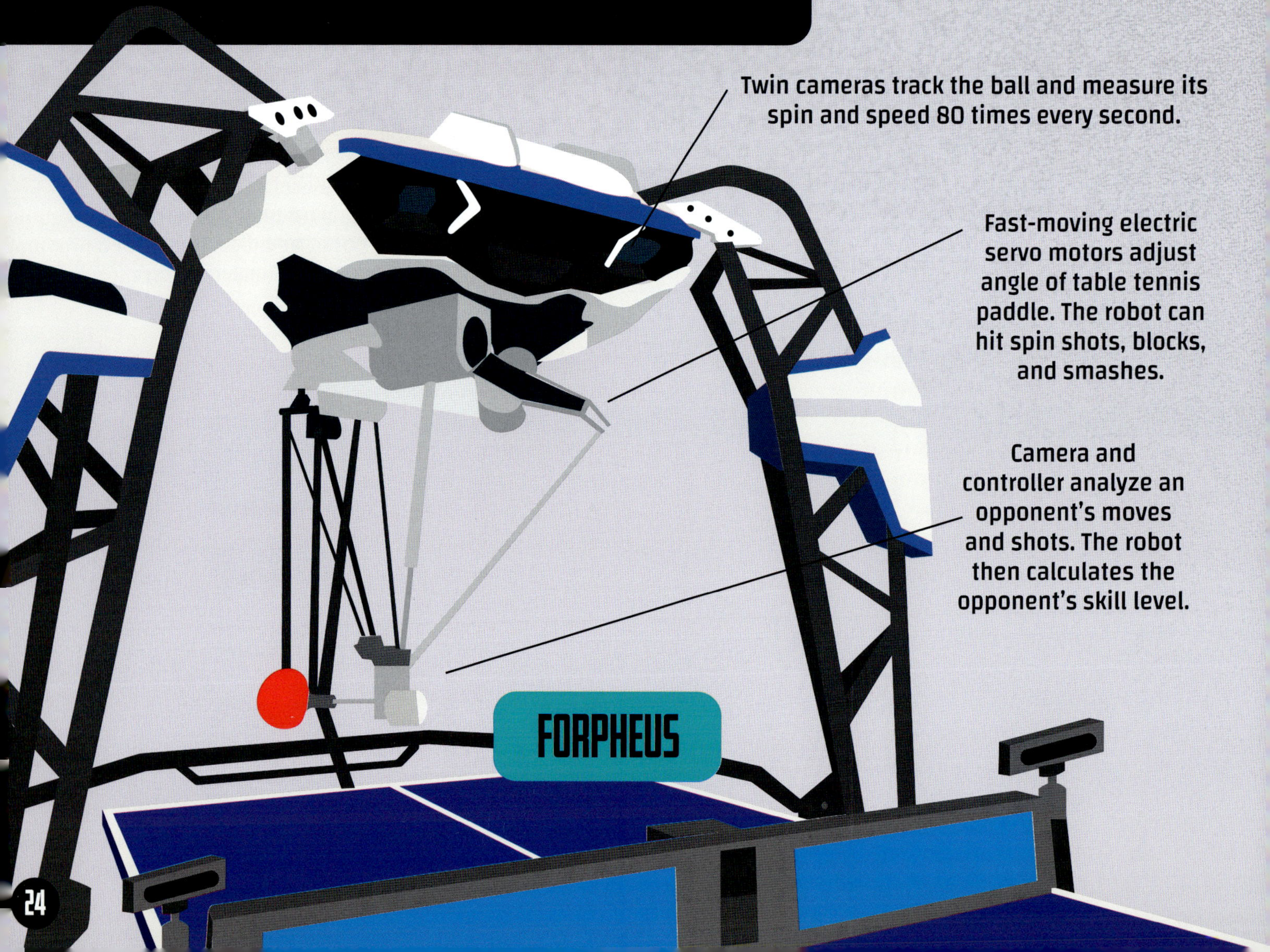

BEATBOT

This prototype robot is designed as a pacer and running companion to athletes in training. It uses nine infrared sensors to follow a line on an athletics track. The athlete can program it using a smartphone to set the speed.

12 FT/S ...

... the speed that the Japanese Volleyball Association's robots' arms move back and forth along the net to block shots to assist human players during practice. The three robotic players can bunch together to block a shot or cover different parts of the net.

2,020 ...

... the number of basketball free throw shots made successfully in a row by Toyota's sharpshooting CUE3 robot in 2019 – a world record. The robot uses sensors in its chest to measure distances to the basket.

130 MPH ...

... the top speed of ELDRIC's golf swing. This robot golfer, named after professional golfer Eldrick "Tiger" Woods, played the 16th hole at the Scottsdale PGA golf course in 2016 and scored a hole in one.

18 SECONDS ...

... the time it took the 30-inch (75 cm)-high robot skier Taekwon V to ski round a slalom course to win an eight-robot skiing competition held in South Korea in 2018. The robot could adjust its 21 joints to shift balance and turn in and out of the slalom gates.

CAREBOTS

More and more people worldwide are in need of care and assistance in medical facilities or in their own homes. These include the very elderly, people suffering from dementia and Alzheimer's, and those with disabilities or special needs. Robots are stepping up to get involved in these vital tasks.

SEAL OF APPROVAL

Loneliness can be a big issue for elderly people and those with anxiety. Pets, real and robotic, can reduce stress. A Japanese robot called PARO is modeled on a baby harp seal. It moves its head and flippers, blinks, and makes facial expressions and sounds to provide company and comfort. Sensors embedded in its fur react to touch.

5,000+ ...

... the number of PARO robots worldwide, some 3,000 of which are in Japan.

The United Nations predicts the number of people aged 80 or over will triple to around 426 million by 2050.

If this occurs, many millions more people will be needed to act as caregivers, helping the elderly and infirm.

SOCIABLE STEVIE

Few robots have their own Twitter account or have appeared on the cover of TIME magazine, but then Stevie II is more sociable than most. Built by Akara in Ireland, this robot can chat and interact with care home patients and smiles if given a compliment.

STEVIE II

TAKING THE STRAIN

Nurses and care home staff may have to lift people they look after out of bed, chairs, and wheelchairs 40 times a day – back-breaking work. Robots like Robear take that strain away – gently lifting patients using their powerful electric actuators.

ROBEAR

Robear weighs 309 pounds (140 kg) and can lift 57% of its bodyweight.

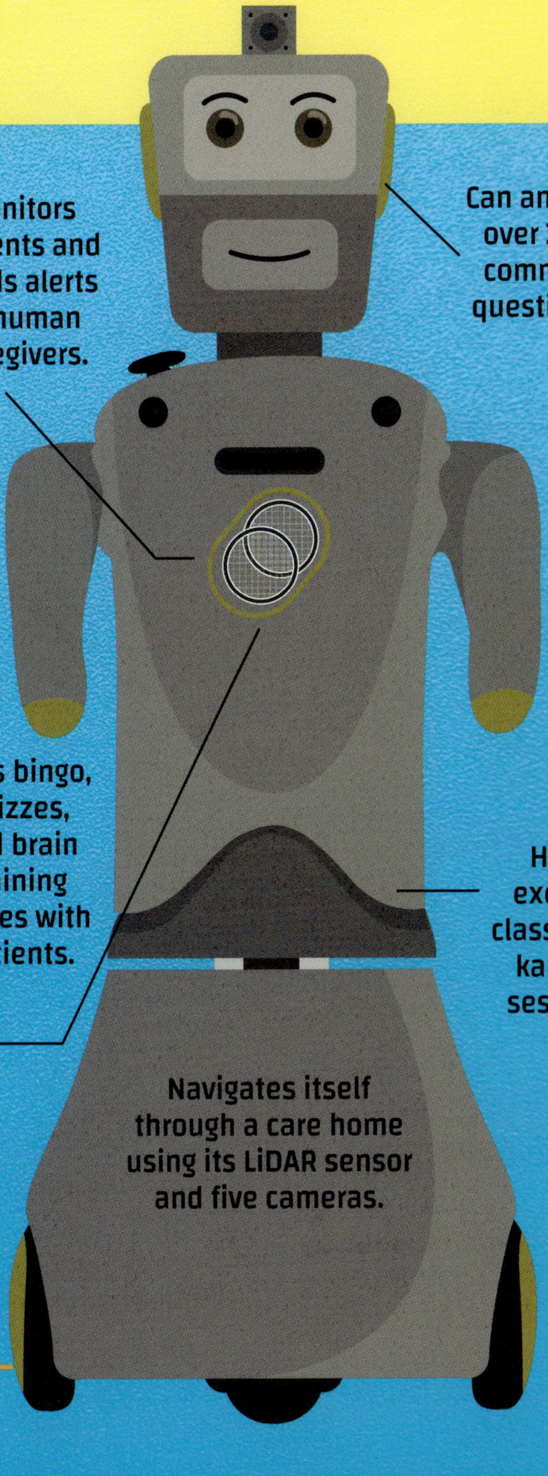

Monitors patients and sends alerts to human caregivers.

Can answer over 100 common questions.

Runs bingo, quizzes, and brain training games with patients.

Holds exercise classes and karaoke sessions.

Navigates itself through a care home using its LiDAR sensor and five cameras.

PILLO

A healthcare personal assistant, Pillo reminds users when to take their medicines and tracks their health care, exercise, and even what they eat. Pillo can hold up to 28 doses of medicine but only dispenses a dose if it recognizes the face of the person.

YOUR ROBOTIC FUTURE

No one knows quite what's in store for service robots and those working in industry in the distant future. One thing is for certain: hundreds of exciting, new robot designs will wow us and some may enter everyday life. Perhaps robot cooks, care workers, and versatile home helpers will be as common in the future as cars and vending machines are today.

WASH AND DRY DROID

Ugo is a prototype laundry handling robot developed in Japan by Mira Robotics. Its vision system works with its grippers to put washing in and take it out of a washing machine and to fold it up neatly when it's dry.

Ugo can effectively kneel down and stand up with its torso and arms rising up and down a vertical rail.

During the COVID-19 pandemic, Ugo was adapted to tackle the virus. Its twin hands were each fitted with a special UV scanner that sends out ultraviolet light to kill the virus.

WORKING TOGETHER

Future breakthroughs may turn thousands of robots into cobots, or collaborative robots. These machines would operate safely alongside people at work and in the home, controlling other “Internet of Things” devices – gadgets and machines connected and controllable via the Internet – such as smart fridges, heating, and other appliances. Future robots may even be able to diagnose and repair each other’s faults!

125,000,000,000 ...

... the number of Internet of Things devices predicted to exist in 2030 – that’s around 15 items for every person on the planet.

129,864,880 ...

... an estimate made by Google of the total number of books ever published. These would take less than 100 terabytes of memory to store – about 20 modern PCs’ worth. Future robots might have all this information and more stored on memory chips.

DRONE TO HOME

Future towns may be buzzing with drones delivering food, packages, and crucial medical supplies more rapidly than by road. In June 2020, a pizza was delivered to a customer on a beach in Zandvoort, the Netherlands, using a robotic drone. Delivery companies and medical responders may use smart drones in the future to whisk important packages to homes in minutes.

One human “pilot” can control up to **10 Flirtey Eagle drones**

The four-engined drone can fly in **95% of weather conditions**

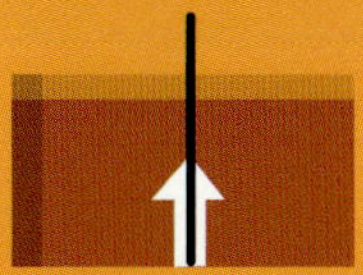

Packages are lowered on a strong tether which automatically unclips once a package is on the ground.

QUIZ

Try this quiz to find out how much you can remember about robot helpers. The answers are at the bottom of the page.

1. Which country has more industrial robots than any other?

a) Germany

b) The United States

c) China

2. On what sort of animal is Paro the care robot modeled?

a) Bear

b) Seal

c) Dog

3. How many operations have da Vinci surgical robots assisted with?

a) 6,000,000

b) 1,500,000

c) 550,000

4. The CUE3 robot made how many successful basketball shots in a row?

a) 150

b) 500

c) 2,020

5. Which of the following tasks has the robot YuMi® not performed?

a) Made paper planes

b) Cooked burgers

c) Conducted an orchestra

6. What is the maximum load that the Canadarm2 can lift in space?

a) 5,291 lb (2,400 kg)

b) 84,878 lb (38,500 kg)

c) 255,736 lb (116,000 kg)

7. Which country has the most industrial robots for every 10,000 of its human workers?

a) Japan

b) South Korea

c) United Kingdom

8. How long does it take for a team of IRB 6640 robot welders to complete 4,000 welds of a car body?

a) 90 seconds

b) 5 minutes

c) 20 minutes

9. How many drumsticks does the Z-Machines' Ashura robot use?

a) 2

b) 6

c) 19

10. How many ultrasonic microphones does the Murata robot have in its head?

a) 2

b) 5

c) 9

Answers

1.c, 2.b, 3.a, 4.c, 5.b, 6.c, 7.b, 8.a, 9.c, 10.b

GLOSSARY

actuator
A device like an electric motor which moves another part.

assembly line
A line of machines and workers in a factory along which a product moves as it is put together.

bacteria
Microscopic, single-celled living things. Some are helpful to human life but others are harmful.

cobots
Short for collaborative robots – machines designed to share information and work together to complete tasks.

controller
The part of the robot which makes decisions and tells the other parts of the robot what to do. It is usually a computer.

database
An organized collection of information which allows data to be easily searched and retrieved.

drone
A pilotless flying machine, usually remote-controlled by a person on the ground.

end effectors
Any device or tool at the end of a robot arm used to interact with the robot's surroundings.

exoskeleton
Tough structures that support the body from the outside.

gyroscopic sensor
A device for measuring and maintaining the position and balance of a robot.

palletizing
To place or stack items on pallets – flat wooden or metal platforms which are easily handled by machines for transport.

pharmacists
People who prepare and dispense drugs and medicines.

sensor
A device that collects information about a robot or its surroundings.

ultrasonic
Describes sound waves that exist above the range of human hearing.

welding
Using heat to join together two pieces of metal or certain types of plastic.

FURTHER INFORMATION

Books

A Robot World – Clive Gifford, Cavendish Square Publishing, 2024

Robots in the Factory – Lisa Idzikowski, Learner Publications, 2024

The Tech-Head Guide: Robots – William Potter, Wayland, 2020

Websites

https://roboticsbiz.com/top-10-greatest-robots-in-sports/
Learn more about robots in sports with text and videos of robots like CUE3 and Forpheus in action.

www.nationalgeographic.com/magazine/2020/09/the-robot-revolution-has-arrived-feature/
A big article on robots and how they may help us in the future.

INDEX